What Is the Sky?

Monica Hughes

Heinemann Library
Chicago, Illinois

Customer Service 888-454-2279
Visit our website at www.heinemannlibrary.com

Page layout by Michelle Lisseter, Heinemann Library
Photo research by Maria Joannou, Erica Newbery, and Kay Altwegg
Printed and bound in China by South China Printing Company

09 08 07 06 05
10 9 8 7 6 5 4 3 2 1

Library of Congress Cataloging-in-Publication Data
Hughes, Monica.
    What is the sky? / Monica Hughes.
        p. cm. -- (The world around us)
    Includes bibliographical references and index.
    ISBN 1-4034-6278-X (lib. bdg.) -- ISBN 1-4034-6284-4 (pbk.)
    1. Sky--Juvenile literature. I. Title. II. Series: Hughes, Monica.
World around us.
    QC863.5.H84 2004
    551.5--dc22

                                        2004014865

Acknowledgments
The publishers would like to thank the following for permission to reproduce photographs: Alamy pp. **7** (John Foxx), **13** (Peter Usbeck), **15** (Image Farm Inc); **21** (Brand X Pictures), **23c** (Peter Usbeck); Corbis (B.S.P.I.) pp. **16**, **22**; Getty Images (Photodisc) pp. **6**, **17**, **22**, **23a**; Harcourt Education Ltd (Corbis) pp. **4**, **8**, **10**, **11**, **14**, **18**, **19**, **20**, **22**, **23d**, **23e**; KPT Power Photos pp. **12**, **23b**; Science Photo Library (David Nunuk) pp. **5**, **9**.

Cover photograph reproduced with permission of Corbis.

Every effort has been made to contact copyright holders of any material reproduced in this book. Any omissions will be rectified in subsequent printings if notice is given to the publisher.
Many thanks to the teachers, library media specialists, reading instructors, and educational consultants who have helped develop the Read and Learn/Lee y aprende brand.

Contents

Some words are shown in bold, **like this**. You can find them in the picture glossary on page 23.

Have You Seen the Sky?

When you are outside, if you look up you will see the sky.

The sky is always above you at the beach or the city.

All over the world the sky is above you.

The sky does not always look the same, though.

What Is the Sky Like in the Day?

The Sun lights up the sky during the day.

Sometimes the sky is bright blue and there are no **clouds**.

Sometimes the sky looks white, or even gray.

There is less light because the clouds hide the Sun.

What Is the Sky Like at Night?

If there are no **clouds** at night, sometimes you can see the **Moon**.

The Moon does not always look the same shape.

The sky is darker at night because the Sun cannot be seen.

Sometimes you can see the light from bright stars.

When Does the Sky Change Color?

Every morning the Sun rises and lights up the sky.

The sky may look red, yellow, or even orange at **sunrise**.

At the end of the day the Sun goes down and night begins.

The sky changes color again when the Sun sets.

How Does the Sky Show the Weather?

Looking at the sky can tell you what the weather will be.

Clear blue skies and thin **clouds** mean a warm, dry day.

Dark gray or black clouds usually bring rain.

Lightning lights up the sky during a thunderstorm.

13

What Falls from the Sky?

Rain falls from gray or black **clouds** in the sky.

After rain, the clouds in the sky are white.

When it is very cold, snow falls from clouds instead of rain.

Snow can be blown across the sky by strong winds.

How Big Is the Sky?

The sky is made of air called the **atmosphere**.

When you look up, you only see part of the sky.

The sky stretches away from Earth into space.

We look through the atmosphere to see the Sun, **Moon**, and stars.

How Do Animals and Plants Use the Sky?

Animals need air to breathe and light and warmth from the Sun.

Birds and insects use the sky to fly around.

Plants need rain from the sky to grow.

Many plants grow upward and turn to face the Sun in the sky.

How Do People Use the Sky?

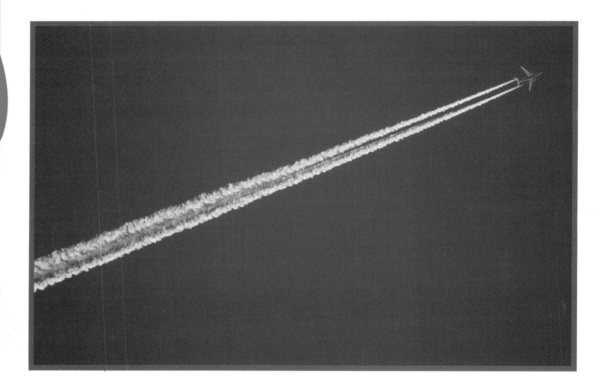

People need air to breathe, just like animals and plants.

We can use the sky to travel from place to place in airplanes.

People also use the sky to have fun.

Skydiving is one way to enjoy the sky!

Quiz

Which of these use the sky?

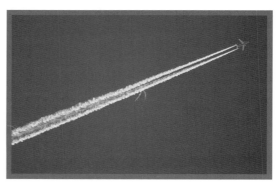

Picture Glossary

atmosphere
pages 16, 17
air or gases surrounding Earth

cloud
pages 6, 7, 8, 12, 13, 14, 15
water vapor that forms white,
gray, or black patches in the sky

lightning
page 13
bright flash of natural electricity
made during a storm

Moon
pages 8, 17
huge object that can usually be
seen in the sky at night

sunrise
page 10
time of day when the Sun comes
up and first appears in the sky

Note to Parents and Teachers

Reading for information is an important part of a child's literacy development. Learning begins with a question about something. Help children think of themselves as investigators and researchers by encouraging their questions about the world around them. Each chapter in this book begins with a question. Read the question together. Look at the pictures. Talk about what you think the answer might be. Then read the test to find out if your predictions were correct. Think of other questions you could ask about the topic, and discuss where you might find the answers. Assist children in using the picture glossary and index to practice vocabulary and research skills.

Index

Answer to Quiz on Page 22

Airplanes and hot air balloons use the sky.